Summary:

Tribe

By: Sebastian Junger

Proudly Brought to you by:

Legal & Disclaimer

provided by this guide. This disclaimer applies to any damages or injury caused by the use and application, whether directly or indirectly, of any advice or information presented, whether for breach of contract, tort, negligence, personal injury, criminal intent, or under any other cause of action.

You agree to accept all risks of using the information presented inside this book. You need to consult a professional medical practitioner in order to ensure you are both able and healthy enough to participate in this program.

Table of Contents

The Book at a Glance

Imagine living in a completely egalitarian community: a world where there's neither social division nor high expectations. To us, living in such a peaceful community has tremendous appeal. But believe it or not, this was how our ancestors used to live. And according to Sebastian Junger, living without these boundaries is one of the most ideal ways to live.

It is a well-known fact that humans are social beings. This means that we derive much of our happiness from the connectedness we experience within the community. However, modern society and industrialization made us put more value on self-reliance and independence – eventually making us lose sight of our humanistic need for brotherhood.

Sebastian Junger, a New York-based journalist who has been deployed to cover war stories, aims to educate us on the negative effects of modernization through this book entitled Tribe. In this book, he shares how American Indian tribes peacefully live their lives, and compares it with how we live our lives today. All information shared in this book is backed by historical facts and well-researched data in order to convincingly drive his point to his readers.

This book is divided into four informative chapters. The first chapter focuses around the unique sense of community which can only be found within tribes. In this chapter, the author highlights that although these tribal men were considered as savages, their seemingly "civilized" prisoners would willingly refuse to return to their families – all because of that unique bond of companionship.

In the second chapter, the author talks about how war, as well as other traumatic experiences, can cause us to revert back to our tribal ways. He explains that during these troubled times, our social boundaries are temporarily gone, and this makes us act selflessly in order to keep each person in the community alive.

Chapter three, on the other hand, discusses the psychological effects of these traumatic experiences upon its survivors and victims. But most importantly, it talks about the alienation which comes from being seen as victims.

And finally, the fourth chapter lays down the ways by which we can help veterans and survivors transition back to the community. In this final chapter, the author enumerates the various ceremonies conducted by American Indian tribes, and discusses why it is an effective tool in the transition process.

Through this book, the author hopes to promote a general sense of brotherhood within various communities: whether it is one which is as highly industrialized as the United States or not. And through the course of reading, readers will be able to pick up historical trivia and facts which can be useful in our everyday lives. Ultimately, this book also seeks to develop an admiration towards the ancient human beings which once roamed the earth. For without their continuous aspiration to improve their way of life, we might not be enjoying the comforts of modern-day society.

As you progress with this book, the author hopes that you keep an open mind so that you can fully appreciate the facts and data presented in this book.

FREE BONUSES

P.S. Is it okay if we overdeliver?

Here at Readtrepreneur Publishing, we believe in overdelivering way beyond our reader's expectations. Is it okay if we overdeliver?

Here's the deal, we're going to give you an extremely condensed PDF summary of the book which you've just read and much more…

What's the catch? We need to trust you… You see, we want to overdeliver and in order for us to do that, we've to trust our reader to keep this bonus a secret to themselves? Why? Because we don't want people to be getting our exclusive PDF summaries even without buying our books itself. Unethical, right?

Ok. Are you ready?

Firstly, remember that your book is code: **"READ129"**.

Next, visit this link: **http://bit.ly/exclusivepdfs**

Everything else will be self explanatory after you've visited: **http://bit.ly/exclusivepdfs**.

We hope you'll enjoy our free bonuses as much as we enjoyed preparing it for you!

The Men And The Dogs

There is no doubt that the United States of America is one of the most powerful nations today. The author shares that what's interesting about America's rise to power is the fact that it became a superpower while also facing an internal battle against its native population.

On one side of the country are the Americans which form part of an ever-changing industrial society where all men are seen as equals – ideally, at least. On the other side were the so-called "Indians" – the Native Americans – who were able to preserve their culture and lifestyle from thousands of years ago. Nonetheless, despite the many technological advances offered in the seemingly modernized part of America, statistics show that these men end up embracing Indian society and culture, but never the other way around.

The author shares that this preference for tribal life was seen as a problem by the whites, especially around the time of the Pennsylvania frontier wars. In 1763, Indian tribes became concerned by the advance of white settlements in their area, which led them to convene with each other. Pontiac, an

Ottawa Indian leader, believed that if all of their tribes would become unified, it would be big enough to push the whites back and stop them from taking more of their land. Known for his oratorical prowess, Pontiac was able to convince the warriors that there was a need to protect their people from these advancing white settlements.

Their attack eventually became an all-out war, with the Indians being able to kill around 2,000 settlers, while threatening the survivors to run away. But unknown to them, the English were also preparing for battle. The Highlander Infantry, led by Colonel Henri Bouquet, were ordered to capture native women and children so that they could be sold into slavery. Bounties were also to be paid to those who could manage to carve any scalp from the head of the Natives.

Within months, Bouquet's army defeated the Indians at Bushy Run and successfully regained control of Fort Pitt and other outlying garrisons. They continued to push forward and eventually penetrated the heart of the Indian Territory. And by mid-October, the Highlanders were met by a delegation of Indians who wanted to end the war and negotiate peacefully. By this time, the Indians were able to imprison several whites, so the first demand from Bouquet was their immediate release. But, what happened next led them to confusion.

In the succeeding weeks after they convened, hundreds of these captives were released and brought to the Highlanders. White relatives flocked to meet their captured loved ones, but only to be met by much reluctance. Some of these captives were too young to remember living within white settlement, so they considered the Indian community their home. Most of the young women, on the other hand, were already married to Indian men and weren't enthusiastic about returning to their families.

This reluctance to leave their adoptive tribe became controversial among the whites. All this time, they believed in their superiority as a highly-industrialized society; yet, the fact their own people decided to stay with the Indians made them question that belief.

Among the first men to understand the underlying reason behind this phenomenon was Hector de Crevecoeur. According to the author, Crevecoeur claimed that the social bond among the Indians may have captivated the English. In fact, he believed that it was far more appealing than the material comforts of civilization.

To further add credence to Crevecoeur's supposition, the

author also shares the story of Mary Jemison, who became a Seneca captive at the age of 15. Being taken from the Pennsylvania frontier at a young age, people would expect her to be terrified of her predicament. But instead, she became enamored with the Seneca way of life that she even hid from an organized search party which was looking to rescue her. Jemison explains that Indians knew how to live happily, and that had drawn her towards that lifestyle.

But of course, the Puritan leaders didn't think of this lightly. They simply couldn't understand why people would willingly turn their back on their civilized Christian society. In fact, they even imposed penalties to anyone who would take side with the Indians. Nonetheless, some frontiersmen still chose to embrace the Indian lifestyle.

At this point, the author reminds us that we shouldn't romanticize the Indian life too much. Enemy tribes would inflict cruel punishment on each other – too cruel that it can even be considered as inhuman in our modern times. But, as cruel as it may seem, the author reminds us that during the Spanish Inquisition, being burned alive was considered as a normal punishment. Thus, although the era was plagued by inhumanities, it was actually considered the norm during that time – and the Indians were no exception. Now, it seems clear that they were improperly referred to as "savages".

Nonetheless, the author shares that the most compelling aspect of native life is its egalitarianism. Within these tribes, wealth was not counted by the amount of personal property one has. Neither was social status attached to these material belongings.

To the native people, success was measured differently. For the men, their success depended on their hunting and war performance. On the other hand, women's independence and sexual freedom were respected. As a result, they bore fewer children than women of their age in white settlements. In fact, the author shares a quote from an anonymous colonial woman who remarked that women in tribes are regarded as equals. They were free to do whatever they pleased, and were not being held back by the expectations of others. To her, this was what it meant to be truly independent – and that independence was truly appealing.

From this feeling of independence, tribal members also developed a sense of loyalty to their community. John Dunn Hunter, a captive of the Kickapoo Nation, shares that tribal members were so loyal that there was never an instance of treason, nor was there a punishment for such disloyalty. It simply did not exist. Cowardice, on the other hand, was severely punished. In effect, members became fiercely loyal and courageous; and the preservation of the tribe was everyone's sacred duty.

But, the author shares that the real question is not why tribal life is so appealing. Instead, he shares that we should look for the answer to why Western civilization is so unappealing.

Theoretically, and on a material level, Western life offers more comfort and protection. However, the downside in relying too much on these material comforts is that when society becomes more affluent, the tendency is to work harder. Industrialization takes much of our time and commitment that we end up spending less time with our loved ones. Thus, the majority of people feel that the value of wealth and safety is far less than the value of freedom.

In the 1960s, a research based on the !Kung people, a nomadic tribe of the Kalahari Desert, revealed that they only needed twelve hours per week in order to survive the desert's harsh conditions. How they manage to survive is because of their cooperative nature. The author shares that members of the !Kung tribe would hunt, gather, and pool all their food which would be shared with the entire community. Sharing – instead of surplus accumulation – is at the heart of their values. And it is because of their ability to share that they were able to survive the harsh Kalahari environment for thousands of years.

Completely contrary to this !Kung lifestyle is how we are living now. With modernization, people end up putting too much value on the accumulation of personal property – all because of a false pretense that it will help them take control of their life.

Unfortunately, property accumulation is doing more harm than good. According to the author, there is enough evidence to prove that this desire to accumulate wealth is one of the main causes for mental illnesses. In fact, cross-cultural research reveals that the increase in affluence and urbanization is directly proportional to the increase in depression and suicide rates. Thus, it seems that modernization and increased wealth only fosters loneliness and clinical depression – the complete opposite of what it promises to achieve.

Nonetheless, suicide is also present among tribal societies. Studies conducted among American Indians reveal that they only commit suicides on certain occasions, like to avoid being a burden to the tribe during old age, experiencing grief after the death of a spouse, losing a battle with the enemy, and to avoid experiencing the agony of torture. There were also

7

some tribes who would prefer to commit suicide than to live a life with a hideously disfigured face due to being afflicted with smallpox.

From these examples, we can see that suicides weren't rooted on psychological causes. In fact, other studies also reveal that certain tribes – the Bella Coola, Ojibwa, Zuni, and Southern Paiute, among others – never experienced suicide at all. But in contrast, modern societies experience suicide at a rate of 25 cases for every 100,000 people.

To further drive his point, the author also shares the results of a survey conducted by the World Health Organization on the subject of depression among wealthy countries. According to this study, people living in wealthy countries are eight times more likely to suffer from depression than those living in poor countries.

From this, the author concludes that the reason behind these statistics is that poor people share their resources, so they live in closer communities. In contrast, the affluent are made to believe that they are self-reliant, but this runs counter to human experience – we are social beings, after all.

At this point, we already have a general overview of what can truly help us live happy lives. And in order to truly guarantee happiness, the author shares the self-determination theory with us.

According to the self-determination theory, humans only need three basic things in life: the need to feel competent, the need to feel authentic, and the need to feel connected. As you may have noticed, these values are all intrinsic. Unfortunately, modern society puts too much emphasis on the extrinsic values of status, money and beauty – the same values which can trigger nasty mental health issues.

It is also worth noting that the affluent experience these alienating effects early on in their lives. In America and Northern European countries, children are made to sleep in separate rooms in order for them to become "self-soothing" when they grow up. But again, this runs counter to our human nature. According to the author, children are supposed to feel a sense of safety only from knowing that their parents are sleeping near them, and this is exactly what hunter-gatherer parents do with their children.

Another factor worth noting is that our modern society also lays emphasis on authority, instead of community. Whenever we feel like we belong in a certain community, we experience increased levels of oxytocin. And when we have more oxytocin in our system, then we also experience an overall sense of happiness and loyalty to the group. Unfortunately, the opposite is true in our modern societies. Instead of fostering loyalty, we end up experiencing fraudulent schemes, betrayals, and bouts of dishonesty – all of which may be severely punishable if we had been living with native tribes.

From all of these comparisons, the author shares that although the tribes lacked scientific and technical know-how, they are the ones who seem to have mastered the art of living happily. More on this topic will be discussed in the succeeding chapters.

War Makes You An Animal

Starting from a young age, the author had always been fascinated with war. According to him, this fascination wasn't just because he was living in wartime – instead, it was because of his belief that his family might not have existed if it wasn't for war.

He shares that his maternal ancestors were German emigrants who fought in the American Revolution. His father, on the other hand, had European roots and immigrated to America to escape the Spanish Civil War. Nonetheless, his father signed up for military service where he was assigned to work with jet engines in New Jersey. This experience caused his father to become greatly antiwar.

But his father's reaction to when he received his selective service card surprised the author. Because the Vietnam War had just ended, the author didn't think it was necessary to enlist in the army. His father lectured him on patriotism – a lecture that opened his eyes to the fact that there was something bigger than himself, and that was something he was willing to fight for.

Drafting men for the war is common in today's modern society. People are made to believe that maintaining a civilized society keeps people away from harm. Ideally, violence was something to be avoided; thus, they weren't encouraged to fight, unless it was completely necessary.

In contrast, tribal societies require young men to go through a form of brutal initiation as a test for adulthood. According to the author, certain tribes would impose seemingly inhuman initiations that some of these young men wound up dead. Thus, tribal youngsters were forced into fights.

The author shares that having these fights forms part of our human nature. He explains that, since modern society boys are no longer thrust into tribal initiation rites, their human nature makes them want to prove their readiness for manhood in various ways. This includes dangerous feats like driving too fast, hazing, joining fraternities, and other dangerous activities. Nonetheless, it is not the violence that draws young men into engaging in these activities – they're actually after the maturity and respect which results from it.

To help us appreciate this idea better, the author shares his own experience in Sarajevo, where he served as a journalist during the civil war when the Serb forces took over Bosnia in 1991. The city was known for its picturesque cafes and galleries, but it was the complete opposite during wartime.

Streets were filled with garbage and destroyed cars, while buildings were peppered with bullet holes. It was a terrible sight. In daytime, citizens would fill the streets to carry water or gather food and firewood. But, as nighttime engulfs the city, it eventually turns into a dark ghost town. How this happened was greatly due to its being surrounded by mountains – with the Serbs attacking from high ground, the city was practically defenseless.

The situation in Sarajevo was so bad that the author recalls that it was a normal sight to see an older person sprawled over the street with a bullet in their forehead. Additionally, Serbs took over the surrounding mountaintops that a major highway was clearly exposed to gunshot, making it impossible for those trapped within the city to leave. And those who tried to leave often didn't make it.

This civil war lasted for three years, and killed or wounded nearly 70,000 people. There were even reported instances when people deliberately exposed themselves to the Serbs because their predicament made them feel miserable.

Among the various situations he witnessed in Sarajevo, what struck him most during this time of societal collapse was how people dealt with each other. For in those moments of hardships, you could truly see that everyone were equals.

The author relates this tragedy to another one which occurred in 1915, when an earthquake struck Avezzano, Italy. The earthquake was of such high magnitude that it killed around 30,000 people – both rich and poor. Those who survived the quake only had survival in mind, so they let go of their societal divide in order to help each other out. This community-oriented behavior, according to the author, is what our modern society needs to promote.

Another example of this behavior can be depicted by the people of London during World War II. During this time, which is particularly known as the London Blitz, the city was among the main targets of aerial bombardments. To remedy the situation, the Churchill government provided its people with public bomb shelters.

Emergency planners, along with the government, thought it would be a bad idea to fit large groups of people into tiny spaces. They feared the worst, and even believed that it might cause an uproar against the government. Fortunately, the opposite was true.

One woman who had lived through the Blitz recalled that, at

that time, everyone was willing to fight against the Germans, even if they were only armed with broken bottles. Instead of not leaving the shelters – which the government had feared – Londoners would leave and head to work in the morning. Additionally, every one lived peacefully with one another that there was no need to summon the police: the crowd would work out ways to pacify themselves.

However, this doesn't mean that the people of London had it easy during the Blitz. Although it seemed that they went on with their daily lives as if nothing was happening, the aerial bombardments they were subjected to wounded – and even killed – thousands of people. The author even shares that the badly wounded would simply be given morphine and left to die, while only those who showed a higher chance for survival were saved.

Accounts from survivors claim that the bombing sounded like a massive marching band parading around the city. The worst accounts, however, described the horrors of how hundreds died in an instant when factories, food manufacturing plant, and underground shelters were directly hit.

During these turbulent times, the government predicted that a psychiatric breakdown would plague England. Again, the opposite was true. Records reveal that these experiences neither triggered mass hysteria nor individual psychosis, and that admissions to psychiatric hospitals were greatly reduced. The author also shares that as the Blitz progressed, long-standing psychiatric patients saw their symptoms go down, and were able to help by driving ambulances. All of these situations show that people did well – in terms of mental health, at least – during wartime.

To further drive his point on the positive effects of war, the author shares the results of a study conducted by renowned sociologist, Emile Durkheim. Durkheim's research reveals that suicide rates dropped whenever countries went to war, like when psychiatric wards throughout Paris remained empty throughout the war. Other researchers also uncovered a similar pattern during various civil wars in Spain, Algeria, Lebanon and Norther Ireland.

H. A. Lyons, an Irish psychologist, also noted the sharp drop of suicide, homicide, and violent crime rates during the 1969 and 1970 riots in Belfast. In contrast, those living in County Derry – which was incredibly peaceful during those times – experienced an increase in depression rates. Lyons attributed this increase in depression rates to feeling useless despite their willingness to help the society. According to him, actively engaging in a cause above their own, their life becomes filled with purpose, thus resulting in an improved state of mental health. Nonetheless, this baffled everyone, because it seemed like violence was a solution for our mental health issues – and that didn't make any sense.

We cannot, however, deny the overwhelming amount of evidence at hand. Going back to the effect of the London Blitz, the author shares that survivors seem to have found a strange feeling of reassurance due to the regularity of the air raids. Apparently, this has also caused Londoners to take action and help the community in their own way.

Other examples of this community-centered behavior are present in areas around the world which suffered from the same tragic fate. In 1961, Charles Fitz conducted a general study on how communities respond to calamities. Numerous data was gathered by his team of expert researchers from conducting interviews of over 9,000 survivors. This study revealed that large-scale disasters reinforce social bonds within communities, which inspires people to promote the good of the community instead of what is just good for themselves. Fritz theorized that, although modern society provides us with many comforts, it actually disrupts this ideal social bond by promoting being self-sufficient. Unfortunately, being self-sufficient ran counter to our natural human ways.

Fritz encourages us to look at disasters as a phenomenon which creates a community of people who are connected by a common threat which they seek to overcome. In these instances, people look beyond class differences and ethnic races, and look at all of them collectively – as a group of human beings. When people experience this unity, it is incredibly gratifying; more so to those suffering from mental illnesses, who find this extremely therapeutic.

This theory was proven afterward on May 31, 1970, when a powerful earthquake struck the city of Yungay, Chile. The quake was strong enough to cause a rockslide which killed around 70,000 people in the region. On the other hand, the ten percent which survived the rockslide was left on their own for days, since the dust from all the rubble made it impossible for rescue helicopters to land. These survivors developed a sense of brotherhood and helped each other survive – regardless of what social class they were in prior to the quake. The sad part about it, however, was that as soon as they were rescued, this sense of brotherhood was lost. They were back in the arms of modern society.

The author shares that this drive to help each other is so great that people are willing to risk their lives for it. However, the author also observed that this risk-taking tendency differs between men and women.

Since time immemorial, men always played the role of the hunter and protector of the community, while women were more concerned with the upbringing and peace within the community. Thus, men experience a sense of accomplishment whenever they perform tasks which keep the community safe, while women were the ones who displayed moral courage. In this sense, women were more likely to sacrifice their lives to help save others.

Statistically speaking, women received more Righteous Among The Nations Awards than men. This award was given to those who were willing to risk their own lives in order to save Jewish lives during the Holocaust. This data reflects the fact that women are, indeed, more likely to take a stand concerning moral and social issues which threaten the community.

The author notes that the two types of courage present in men and women are essential in order for groups to survive life-threatening situations. However, this doesn't mean that men are the only ones who can possess the care-taking courage, while women are the only ones capable of possessing moral courage. Instead, life-and-death situations nudge people into developing these types of courage regardless of gender.

To illustrate, the author shares the story of miners who were trapped in the Springhill Mine in Nova Scotia. On October 23, 1958, the Springhill Mine experienced a contraction of its sedimentary layers which generated an explosion which caused its collapse. Almost instantly, 74 miners were killed. Some of those who managed to survive were the ones who weren't deep into the mines that they were able to exit safely. Unfortunately, there were around 19 men who were trapped in the mine shaft located 12,000 feet below the ground.

These trapped men had no food or water – not even enough battery to fuel their lights. Communicating with those above ground was also impossible. Although the Miner's Code made their rescue certain, they had no idea how long such rescue would take. They knew that they had to do something in order to survive while waiting for the team of rescuers.

During this time, certain men already took on leadership roles. Some of them were on the lookout for passageways which could possibly help them escape, while others looked for sources of food or water. However, when their escape attempts failed, a new set of leaders emerged. These new leaders were the ones who gave them hope and encouraged them to stay calm despite their disheartening predicament.

The author explains that the first kind of leaders were those who exhibited the caretaking courage, while the second kind of leaders showed moral courage. Since mining is a predominantly-male industry, this example makes it easier for us to see that the types of courage are interchangeable between the two sexes. Thus, if the situation calls for women to step in and perform the role of the caretaker, they would do so with no hesitation. The same is true for men who feel the need to provide moral support, like in the previous example.

Another important point that the author wishes to share with us is that the effects of these catastrophes remain with the survivor for decades. On one occasion, the author recalls talking to a Sarajevo siege survivor who now works as a taxi driver. The survivor animatedly narrated the story of how he once slipped through enemy lines during the siege – a stark comparison to what he is doing now.

Nonetheless, not all survivors looked at the war with much favor. Another survivor was Nidžara Ahmetašević, who was only seventeen when the war broke out. She was one of the unlucky people who got hit by a shrapnel and had to spend her days in crutches. Initially, Ahmetašević looked back on the war with much disgust. But, something about the war made her feel nostalgic.

Ahmetašević shared that life during wartime involved living in communal apartment buildings where around sixty families would share whatever they had. Sharing was so integral to survival that it had become a way of life for everyone. In fact, she recalls that when she received a single egg for her eighteenth birthday, she had to think of ways to share it with her friends. She also recalls that teenagers shared a basement in one of the buildings, which completely separated them from the adults. In that tiny basement, they ate, laughed, played, and listened to music together. And according to Ahmetašević, that was one of the most liberating moments of her life.

However, her communal life had to end because her parents felt that her chance for survival – since it seemed like her recovery was taking too much time – was low. Her parents sent her to Italy where, indeed, she was able to fully recover. But life in Italy was lonelier than life in the war-torn city. She kept worrying about her parents, her friends, and the community she shared apartments with. Thus, she returned to Bosnia as soon as she had the chance.

The logical thing to do for people who were evacuated from

war-torn areas was to move forward with their new life and never look back. But Ahmetašević did the exact opposite. She explains that she went back because she missed being around people. True enough, war makes you an animal. But since we're all animals, it was then that she was at her happiest.

In Bitter Safety I Awake

As mentioned in the previous chapter, the effects of war stay with the survivor for decades. The problem, however, is that they don't always realize it until they become an emotional mess. At least, this was the case for the author.

The author shares that he was oblivious about this problem, until he was back in New York after spending two months in Afghanistan. Being in Afghanistan led the author to witness traumatic incidents – casualties, bomber jets hovering overhead, and other horrifying wartime scenarios. But, he stopped thinking about all of these as soon as he returned home. He was just grateful to be back.

A few months later, while he was onboard the subway, he began to see things from a different perspective. Suddenly, it was as if everything around him posed as a threat: the train was moving too fast, and that the world was too chaotic and loud. At that moment, he was convinced that death was upon him soon.

The fact that he was scared of an impending death while

riding the subway bothered the author a lot. He was far more frightened on that trip than he ever was while in Afghanistan. Unfortunately for him, that train ride began his rollercoaster ride with panic attacks, especially when he was confined in overcrowded spaces. Living with these panic attacks lasted for months, until he met a psychotherapist who convinced him that what he had was post-traumatic stress disorder or PTSD.

Luckily, what he had was merely short-term PTSD. The author shares that this is usually the case for people who have gone through traumatic experiences. In his case, it was his time in Afghanistan which really triggered the disorder.

The author, however, tries to make us understand PTSD from an evolutionary perspective. He explains that this is our natural human reaction to dangerous situations. Human beings tend to become more vigilant when confronted with danger, and this vigilance often makes us both angry and depressed. He explains that anger makes us ready to fight, while depression keeps us from putting ourselves in more danger. Thus, these emotions are all part of our natural defense mechanism.

The effects of PTSD, fortunately, weaken with the passage of time. For the author, his panic attacks eventually ceased, but an overwhelming emotionality replaced it. He recalls tearing up over the smallest details, or being engulfed in sorrow after having a bad dream.

At this point, the author decides to share the story of his friend, Joanna, with us. In the 1960s, Joanna helped black voters register in the South – an act which, at that time, could get her killed. But despite that danger, she still pursued her cause.

The author shares that Joanna's willingness to sacrifice her life for others made him emotionally break down. The same was true when he would listen to stories about soldiers bravely facing the enemy. Any story that would remind him of how human beings are willing to sacrifice their lives for others would practically make him tear up.

To him, this was the effect of war, and it is all too real. This made him realize that war wasn't bad in all aspects. In fact, the author claims that if war is as bad as people claim it to be, then it would not happen as often. Additionally, he also attributes the virtues of loyalty, selflessness, and courage to be the effects of war – virtues which naturally form part of our ancient human genetics, but had been suppressed by modern society.

Among the first people to understand the transformative power of war was the Iroquois Nation. This nation developed a parallel system of government which included two types of leaders. The first group of leaders was the peacetime leaders, called sachems, who led the tribe during times of peace. The second group, on the other hand, was the war leaders who would take over as soon as war breaks out. But, as soon as the enemy suggests peaceful negotiations, then the sachems would again take over.

From this, we can see that the sachems only concerned themselves with justice and fairness among the people and within tribes. In contrast, the war leaders only concerned themselves with the physical protection of their civilian population. According to the author, this is the ideal system of government since it shifts the leadership priorities depending on whether it's wartime or peacetime.

Unfortunately, the opposite is true in these modern times. Often, the civilian population is so isolated from the happenings of war that they are clueless as to the gravity of the situation. In effect, only the soldiers have to switch between peacetime and wartime, and this switch can be stressful sometimes.

The author shares that this alienation that soldiers feel after

27

returning home is best described by a poem written by Siegfried Sassoon entitled, Sick Leave. In the poem, Sassoon describes returning with the following words: "In bitter safety I awake, unfriended. And while the dawn begins with slashing rain, I think of the Battalion in the mud."

This quote from the poem is especially true to soldiers who return home to a healthy and loving response back home. They were often treated as heroes. However, this was confusing to them, because they couldn't see anything heroic about inflicting pain – or killing – another human being. To them, the experience had been extremely traumatic.

Of course, this doesn't mean that the Iroquois warriors never experienced trauma. They did. The difference lies in the fact that the Iroquois Nation, as a whole, experiences the same kind of trauma. Thus, this collective experience within the community makes it possible for them to recover rapidly from the mental tortures of war.

According to study conducted in 2011, violent and aggressive Burundi children were the ones with the lowest PTSD rates. The data, according to the author, reveals that aggression buffers the effects of previous traumatic experience. And since trauma recovery depends on societal factors, the speed at which combat vets recover can be a reliable gauge as to the health of a society.

From a scientific perspective, everyone reacts to trauma by having some sort of acute PTSD. This is a common reaction among mammals, since it helps them defend themselves and avoid danger. However, what people of modern times usually develop is the long-term PTSD, which is relatively uncommon.

Recent studies reveal that out of all people who suffer from traumatic experiences, around twenty percent of them will develop long-term PTSD. The effect of this long-term disorder, however, creates the opposite of its short-term counterpart: sufferers become poorly-adjusted to everyday life.

To drive home the point, the author shares data gathered from a 1992 experiment involving rape victims. We all know that rape is psychologically devastating for its victims, and this is reflected by the fact that about one hundred percent of its survivors show signs of extreme trauma. Nonetheless, the same study reveals that almost half of these survivors experience a significant decline in their trauma within a span of weeks or months.

Statistics likewise show that rape victims tend to recover

faster than soldiers. The author explains that the trauma of being at war is closely interwoven with positive experiences, and it is that aspect that's making it hard for war vets to let go of.

Studies also reveal that persons who develop long-term PTSD were already suffering from psychological issues prior to going into war. The author discusses that the source of these issues vary from person to person, with the most common causes being genetics, or being abused as children. Other contributory factors include being female, having low IQ, or not getting proper education.

Relatedly, suicide is also considered as an expression of PTSD. However, no research data is yet available to clearly delineate the relationship between suicide and combat. In fact, current data shows that veterans who went into war are as likely to commit suicide as those who didn't.

All this information eventually led people to look at battlefield trauma from a different perspective. Since then, it has been rightly categorized as a new kind of trauma. And at the moment, records reveal that the US military has the highest PTSD rates in history.

Nonetheless, the author is not convinced with the statistics.

He avers that these numbers are based merely on the disability claims filed by combat veterans, and that these claims may be based on hearing loss, tinnitus, and PTSD. But, since the grounds for tinnitus and PTSD can be exaggerated or faked, this kind of system could ultimately lead to cases of misdiagnosis. Thus, it may result in erratic statistics.

Another notable thing about combat trauma is that soldiers are not the only ones who suffer from it. Studies reveal that the same effects are experienced by civilian survivors, journalists, Peace Corps members, and other persons who were there, despite not actually fighting on the front lines.

Fortunately, recovery is possible. As previously mentioned, the speed at which a person recovers from PTSD depends greatly on the society they belong to. Unfortunately, modern society doesn't understand the hardships on the battlefield, so instead of feeling the warmth of returning home, these veterans often feel alienated. This, according to the author, is the reason why some war vets claim that they miss the war.

From a clinical perspective, however, this feeling of alienation is different from PTSD. But since it is often experienced combat vets who served abroad, then it is often misdiagnosed as PTSD.

This alienation must not be viewed in a way that would make these veterans look like they are pro-violence. Instead, the author explains that what they actually miss is the unity which is brought about by these traumatic times. In fact, gunner Win Stracke shares that it was one of the best times of his life, since there was an absence of unhealthy competition and boundary.

Thus, as soon as they return to their homes, the expectations and boundaries set by modern society come creeping back. Even when they are back with their loving family, this does not provide them with the same sense of tribalism which they experienced in the military.

The author describes life in the military as one without any sense of privacy. Ten men were often assigned to a hut, which is often only furnished with bunk beds. These bunks were so close to each other that the author recalls being able to touch three persons whenever he would stretch out his arms. In that tiny hut, they practically did everything together. But it was in that tiny space wherein they felt the safest – because they were all part of a group.

Group sleeping is something we have evolved from. The author explains that our ancient ancestors had always practiced group sleeping, because it gave them a sense of companionship and safety. In fact, studies conducted on injured lab rats show that they recover from trauma at a faster rate when they are caged with other rats. Modern society, however, encourages us to become private individuals, thus explaining the slow recovery rates.

As previously mentioned, the proximity of the public to the actual combat also helps speed up the recovery process. According to a study conducted by Dr. Arieh Shalev, people residing in a community which is in close proximity to the battlefield completely understand what the soldiers have experienced. There is no sense of alienation because they know exactly how their warriors felt, and that alone was enough to reduce the latter's stress.

This feeling of companionship was dubbed as the shared public meaning of war. When the public truly understands what vets have gone through, it feels like an acknowledgement of their efforts. And it is this simple acknowledgement which creates a big impact: it makes them feel less futile that they have returned home.

In contrast, societies living away from the chaotic areas would welcome their soldiers with messages of thanks, discounts, and special services. However, this kind of treatment only makes them realize that not everyone serves their country, thereby breeding a sense of alienation.

The author also explains that the way modern society treats its veterans has something to do with its desire to eliminate violence and trauma. Since violence and trauma are seen from a negative perspective, people who tend to experience them are seen as victims. This identity of victimhood, however, greatly delays the recovery process.

Apparently, when aid organizations provide relief to these combatants, the former sends a message that the latter are victims, that they should feel a certain way, and that they will be receiving supplies which are necessary for their survival. Unknown to these aid organizations, combatants never viewed themselves in that way, so these messages of victimhood often only leads them to confusion. Although the intention of these aid organizations is for the good of the combatants, it seems to make matters worse for the latter.

Thus, modern societies glamorize the return of their veterans too much so that they fail to provide them with what they truly need in order to recover from the trauma. In contrast, tribes tend to look at their warriors' return as part of their maturation process, so no alienation takes place at all.

To conclude this chapter, the author shares the following

factors which greatly affect a combatant's recovery:

1. An egalitarian society promotes the mitigation of the effects of trauma, while modern society promotes alienation.

2. Making combatants feel like victims only reduces their chance at speedy recovery.

3. These combatants must feel that they are both necessary and productive when they return.

Calling Home From Mars

The author opens this chapter with a story about one of his visits to Pamplona, Spain. One night, while he was out drinking with a friend at a local pub, three Moroccan men approached their table and claimed that the Viking hat worn by his friend had been stolen from them.

Soon enough, a brawl started between his friend and these men. All of them had a tight grip on the hat as if it was a priceless treasure. Of course, it was such a sight to see at the bar.

When they noticed that it was about to get ripped into pieces, they suddenly calmed down and stopped pulling away from each other. Their hands, however, were still perched on the hat, which serves as a gentle claim of ownership. His friend then called the bartender and asked to have the hat filled with red wine. They agreed to let go of the hat, and to drink from it instead. His friend handed the hat first to the most aggressive one in the group, who drank from it before handing it to the person sitting on his left.

As soon as the hat was empty, they would ask the bartender for another fill. And to cut this story short, the night ended with stories and merriment and the Viking hat controversy had been completely forgotten.

The author shares that he is so fond of this story because he believes that it is reflective of male conflict and closeness. As depicted in the story above, a slight change in the details can ultimately become a unifying factor. From this, the author concludes that there seems to be great human potential based on a sense of brotherhood, and that focusing on our similarities with others tend to put an end to conflicts.

But, in order to live in a society that's conflict-free, there are several factors which we must consider.

When you look at modern society from the perspective of convenience, then there is no doubt that it is an ideal place to live in. Compared to our ancient ancestors, we no longer have to hunt or grow our own food, nor do we have to live with a looming fear that wild animals are to attack us. Additionally, we live in a world that's so scientifically advanced that we are no longer ignorant about the world around us. In fact, even the poorest members of our society enjoy comforts which seemed unimaginable to the ancient human beings.

However, modernization has its costs. With the rise of industrialization, we became focused on developing more ways to make life more convenient. This means more time devoted to working, and less time for connecting with the people around us. Thus, our sense of community was lost.

According to the author, there are two behaviors which set human beings apart from other primates: systematic food sharing, and altruistic self-defense. In fact, he believes that these two behaviors were responsible in leading our early ancestors into building the modern society that it is today.

Of course, human beings still interact with each other. However, this is not the same as the ancient definition for community or tribe, which is a group of people whom you feed and defend. Thus, if we merely have a group of people, it is all merely political – no bond of brotherhood or companionship.

Our modern soldiers, on the other hand, were capable of experiencing this tribal way of thinking when they were sent to war. Sadly, they are also the ones to realize that the tribe they were sacrificing their lives for wasn't willing to make the same sacrifice for them. And that can be truly disheartening.

Nonetheless, the author also points out the fact that this

tribal mindset is also present among other American workers. In fact, these workers perform equally dangerous jobs in certain industries which also make a huge impact upon the community. For example, construction workers sacrifice their own safety in order to build sturdy structures, yet their sacrifice isn't always given recognition. The author attributes this lack of connectedness to society's raising of standards. Those who work in posh offices are the ones whom society considers as successful, while those who are toiling their way under the sun are frowned upon.

The absence of this tribal connectedness has caused us to become incredible self-centered. According to Rachel Yehuda, this selfishness is displayed in the simple act of littering. She explains that when we don't mind creating a mess around us, it means that we are not really thinking about how others will react to that mess. On the other hand, the author added that large-scale self-centeredness is reflected in fraudulent transactions involving millions – if not billions – of dollars.

Littering or fraud, however, does not compare to committing violence against people. To the author, this is the ultimate act of disaffiliation. This act of disaffiliation also existed during ancient times, and was so upsetting to a tribe that a myth was made out of it.

According to the myth, when the Navajo Nation was confined to a reservation in the 1860s, they worried that their warriors would no longer be needed. Out of this thought arose a fear that their warriors would use their skills against their own tribe. They called these fallen warriors as the "skinwalkers".

Stories depict skinwalkers as men who wore the fur of a sacred animal, from which they would gain their powers from. They were believed to have the ability to travel at superhuman speed, and have glowing eyes which could kill in an instant. The thought of having a member of your own tribe try to kill you was so terrifying to the Navajo Nation that they were still scared of them when the author visited them in 1983.

Nonetheless, a similar myth is present in almost every culture around the world, like the werewolves of Europe. But if we try to dissect these myths, we can see that all of them portray one of humanity's most basic fears: that although we can defend ourselves from enemy tribes, we become vulnerable to the attacks of someone from within the community.

The author goes on to discuss that in the Anglo-American

culture, the real threat lies in its growing amount of rampages since the early 1980s. A rampage is defined as an attack made by a lone aggressor against a random group of individuals. Usually, these gunmen kill more than four persons in one place; thus, they can possibly be considered as modern-day skinwalkers.

But if we are to look at the statistics, we will notice that rampages often occur within a certain type of community. For example, these attacks never really happened in urban ghettos – a place which is often depicted by media as a crime-ridden place. Instead, data reveals that these shootings often occur in predominantly-white communities. In fact, they often happen in areas near schools which are within a neighborhood having low crime rates and of affluent families.

These rampage killers are considered as psychopaths, so the fact that they usually come from peaceful and affluent neighborhoods leaves people baffled. In contrast, however, people who come from seemingly dangerous neighborhoods rarely pull out their guns and aimlessly fire at their neighbors. When all these factors are taken together, we begin to question whether living in a perfectly peaceful community is actually good for us or not.

Another factor that the author wishes to add into the picture is that the rate of these killings seem to have dropped during world war, but have been on the rise again since the 1980s. As discussed in the previous chapter, war can bring people together, and that fact is reflected in the decline of rampage killings during those times.

Additionally, the author attributes these killings to the fact that the middle-class Americans already lost their sense of unity. After all, when people live in harmony with each other, the chance for a single psychopath to feel alienated – and eventually attack the community – is greatly reduced, if not avoided completely.

Further digging into research data, the author reveals that the last time when the whole United States experienced a sense of unity was during the September 11 attacks. Two years subsequent to these attacks, authorities report a noticeable drop in crime rates, suicides, and psychiatric disturbances. This was particularly true in New York City, where there was a 20-percent drop in suicide rates and a 40-percent drop in murder rates – all within a span of six months after the attacks. Local pharmacists also report a sudden decline in people asking for antidepressant and antianxiety medications.

Nonetheless, all these factors only seem to make it more complicated for us to understand what is missing in our modern-day living. The author shares that in order to determine what's missing, we have to closely examine which specific behaviors are triggered when life seems to be out of balance.

At this point, the author shares the story of Gregory Gomez. Gomez is an Apache Indian who served in the Vietnam War. Gomez describes the distance between home and the war zone as being in a completely different planet – it was as if he was calling his loved ones from Mars.

Gomez reported that there was a great number of American Indians who served during the Vietnam War, but it wasn't because of their allegiance to the United States government. In fact, he enlisted in the army for a simple reason: because he was a warrior. And true enough, the same was the reason for almost all of the other Indian Americans who went to fight in the war.

Additionally, statistics reveal that American Indians dominate the army, and that they far outnumber all other demographic groups. The author explains that this is owing to the fact that their culture had always considered war as an important step towards maturity and adulthood. Of course, these traditions no longer exist, but the lingering principles still stand – out of which we can all learn from.

Gomez shares that as soon as he returned home from the war, he went into hiding for almost a decade. He felt like he was merely living a normal life, until he realized that he'd been traveling from place to place without remembering why or how we got there. At that point, he was convinced that he needed help: both from a therapist and from undergoing traditional Indian rituals.

The ritual which he joined was called the Sun Dance, which was a traditional Lakotah ceremony wherein dancers would have wooden skewers piercing through the skin on their chests. Their dance would last for hours, ultimately ending when these skewers are finally tear free from the skin. Of this experience, Gomez claims to have been overwhelmed by a feeling of euphoria and strength. And true enough, that's when his healing began.

Of course, different tribes have different opinions about war. For example, the Cheyenne views war as an instrument in proving the honor and courage of their men, while the Papago considered it as a form of insanity. Nonetheless, all of these tribes have varying war-based rituals which, if studied closely, have similar purposes.

Since war was considered as a form of insanity for the Papago, the men returning from war were forced to undergo a form of purification ritual which usually lasts for sixteen days. What's interesting about this purification ritual is that the entire community joins in, based on the belief that every member of the tribe has been affected by the war. And as soon as the ceremony ends, these warriors were then considered to be more superior than those who never went to war.

This kind of togetherness makes it impossible for their warriors as soon as they return home. It also provides them with a strong sense of fulfillment, since they genuinely feel the community's gratitude for their brave acts. Seeing how effective these rituals are in welcoming their warriors back into civilization, American Indian veterans would often turn to these rituals to help them with their transition.

Of course, the author recognizes that the United States is a secular society which cannot just borrow a specific culture's tradition and impose it upon the rest of its citizens. Instead, the author lays emphasis on the spirit of community and healing which can be used to help survivors and victims in transitioning back to normal life. Ceremonies, after all, were created as a means for people to share their experiences with others – and this is true regardless of which culture a certain ceremony belongs to.

From all of these, the author concludes that war veterans and survivors ultimately need a means to vent out their feelings to the community. He observed that modern society, unfortunately, rarely provides them with an opportunity to do so. There are limited instances, like being given the opportunity to speak in front of a crowd about their experiences on Veterans Day, but this often isn't enough. Sometimes, these vets become so emotional that they become unable to share their wartime stories.

Nonetheless, the author recognizes that these community ceremonies can be a stepping stone towards helping these honorable men in transitioning back to the community. After all, what they really need are people who are willing to listen to their experiences – a group of people who understand their hardships and who are truly grateful for their sacrifices.

To conclude this chapter, the author shares that the secret to unifying a secure, wealthy, and modern society is to highlight the fact that we are all human beings. When we stop looking at our differences and focus on this shared humanity, we forget about our boundaries and divisions. We become united as one tribe.

Conclusion

The feeling that we belong to a community is one of the most amazing things we can ever experience as human beings. Being the social beings that we are, we often gain support and inspiration whenever we are surrounded by the people we love.

This sense of longing for companionship and brotherhood is part of our human genetics. As early as thousands of years ago, human beings knew that if they were to survive they had to live in tribes – a community of people who share food and help defend each other. And since human beings are naturally made for tribal life, it cannot be denied that we can be in our happiest and most fulfilled state when we are a part of a tribe.

However, our sense of community is no longer the same as our ancestors'. Modern society not only improved our way of life, but it has also changed our priorities. We are no longer the group of people who would spend a great amount of time with the tribe, while hunting and gathering only took a few hours a week. Instead, we are now a group of people who are willing to spend hours on a job, just to secure a decent pay check which will be used to buy items which we probably would never have enough time to enjoy. And the worst part about industrialization is that we never get enough time to truly connect with the community.

Although we may consider ourselves sociable for having a loving family and a big circle of friends, this is still not the definition of community in a tribal sense. In fact, it can't even be sufficient to be considered a tribe.

The author shares that it is still possible for tribes to exist in these modern times. Groups of people have already experienced this feeling brotherhood that is unique to tribal cultures. However, it only makes itself known to us during times of extreme tragedy. For example, soldiers and civilians experience this bond during wartime, and disaster survivors experience this while they wait for their rescuers to arrive.

The beauty in these traumatic experiences is that it leads people to think beyond themselves. Survivors learn to share their resources, help each other survive, and protect the community. In fact, most of them even report a willingness to risk their own lives for the sake of the community. It is believed, however, that the most beautiful aspect of tribal life is that it eliminates everything that modern society created: personal status, wealth, and social division.

Unfortunately, this sense of community would be cut-short once modern society regains control of the situation. Almost instantaneously, personal and social barriers have gone up again. Soldiers, on the other hand, are made to think that they are victims because tragedies are seen as unfortunate ordeals which no one should go through. Thus, instead of feeling a sense of fulfillment, they feel extremely alienated and victimized.

Nonetheless, these examples reveal that we can still develop that tribal sense of community despite living in modern times. In fact, studies suggest that there are two behaviors which define tribal brotherhood: sharing selflessly, and the willingness to sacrifice one's life for others. Thus, even with the comforts of contemporary technology, as long as we focus on promoting these two behaviors, then we can experience genuine tribal brotherhood in these modern times.

As social beings, we are meant to live with a tribe, after all.

FREE BONUSES

P.S. Is it okay if we overdeliver?

Here at Readtrepreneur Publishing, we believe in overdelivering way beyond our reader's expectations. Is it okay if we overdeliver?

Here's the deal, we're going to give you an extremely condensed PDF summary of the book which you've just read and much more...

What's the catch? We need to trust you... You see, we want to overdeliver and in order for us to do that, we've to trust our reader to keep this bonus a secret to themselves? Why? Because we don't want people to be getting our exclusive PDF summaries even without buying our books itself. Unethical, right?

Ok. Are you ready?

Firstly, remember that your book is code: **"READ129"**.

Next, visit this link: **http://bit.ly/exclusivepdfs**

Everything else will be self explanatory after you've visited: **http://bit.ly/exclusivepdfs**.

We hope you'll enjoy our free bonuses as much as we enjoyed preparing it for you!